Cram101 Textbook Outlines to accompany:

Business Ethics : Managing Corporate Citizenship and Sustainability in the Age of Globalization

Andrew Crane, 2nd Edition

A Content Technologies Inc. publication (c) 2011.

STUDYING MADE EASY

This Cram101 notebook is designed to make studying easier and increase your comprehension of the textbook material. Instead of starting with a blank notebook and trying to write down everything discussed in class lectures, you can use this Cram101 textbook notebook and annotate your notes along with the lecture.

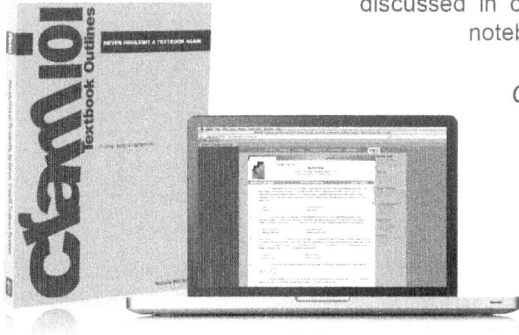

Our goal is to give you the best tools for success.

For a supreme understanding of the course, pair your notebook with our online tools. Should you decide you prefer Cram101.com as your study tool,

we'd like to offer you a trade...

Our Trade In program is a simple way for us to keep our promise and provide you the best studying tools, regardless of where you purchased your Cram101 textbook notebook. As long as your notebook is in *Like New Condition**, you can send it back to us and we will immediately give you a Cram101.com account free for 120 days!

Let The *Trade In* Begin!

THREE SIMPLE STEPS TO TRADE:

1. Go to www.cram101.com/tradein and fill out the packing slip information.

2. Submit and print the packing slip and mail it in with your Cram101 textbook notebook.

3. Activate your account after you receive your email confirmation.

* Books must be returned in *Like New Condition*, meaning there is no damage to the book including, but not limited to; ripped or torn pages, markings or writing on pages, or folded / creased pages. Upon receiving the book, Cram101 will inspect it and reserves the right to terminate your free Cram101.com account and return your textbook notebook at the owners expense.

Learning System

Cram101 Textbook Outlines is a learning system. The notes in this book are the highlights of your textbook, you will never have to highlight a book again.

How to use this book. Take this book to class, it is your notebook for the lecture. The notes and highlights on the left hand side of the pages follow the outline and order of the textbook. All you have to do is follow along while your instructor presents the lecture. Circle the items emphasized in class and add other important information on the right side. With Cram101 Textbook Outlines you'll spend less time writing and more time listening. Learning becomes more efficient.

Cram101.com Online

Increase your studying efficiency by using Cram101.com's practice tests and online reference material. It is the perfect complement to Cram101 Textbook Outlines. Use self-teaching matching tests or simulate in-class testing with comprehensive multiple choice tests, or simply use Cram's true and false tests for quick review. Cram101.com even allows you to enter your in-class notes for an integrated studying format combining the textbook notes with your class notes.

Visit **www.Cram101.com**, click Sign Up at the top of the screen, and enter **DK73DW12149** in the promo code box on the registration screen. Your access to www.Cram101.com is discounted by 50% because you have purchased this book. Sign up and stop highlighting textbooks forever.

Business Ethics : Managing Corporate Citizenship and Sustainability in the Age of Globalization
Andrew Crane, 2nd

CONTENTS

Chapter 1. Introducing business ethics

Universal Declaration of Human Rights	The Universal Declaration of Human Rights is a declaration adopted by the United Nations General Assembly on 10 December 1948 at the Palais de Chaillot in Paris. The Declaration has been translated into at least 375 languages and dialects, making it the most widely translated document in the world. The Declaration arose directly from the experience of the Second World War and represents the first global expression of rights to which all human beings are entitled.
Sweatshop	Sweatshop is a working environment considered to be unacceptably difficult or dangerous -- particularly by industrialized nations with high standards of living. However Sweatshops may exist in any country. Sweatshop workers often work long hours for unusually low pay, regardless of laws mandating overtime pay or a minimum wage.
Child labour	Child labour refers to the employment of children at regular and sustained labour. This practice is considered exploitative by many international organizations and is illegal in many countries. Child labour was utilized to varying extents through most of history, but entered public dispute with the advent of universal schooling, with changes in working conditions during the industrial revolution, and with the emergence of the concepts of workers` and children`s rights.
Millennium Development Goals	The Millennium Development Goals are eight international development goals that all 192 United Nations member states and at least 23 international organizations have agreed to achieve by the year 2015. They include reducing extreme poverty, reducing child mortality rates, fighting disease epidemics such as AIDS, and developing a global partnership for development. In 2001, recognizing the need to assist impoverished nations more aggressively, UN member states adopted the targets. The Millennium Development Goalss aim to spur development by improving social and economic conditions in the world`s poorest countries.
Room	A Room, in architecture, is any distinguishable space within a structure. Usually, a Room is separated from other spaces or passageways by interior walls; moreover, it is separated from outdoor areas by an exterior wall, sometimes with a door. Historically the use of Rooms dates at least to early Minoan cultures about 2200 BC, where excavations on Santorini, Greece at Akrotiri reveal clearly defined Rooms within certain structures.

Chapter 1. Introducing business ethics

Kyoto Protocol	The Kyoto Protocol is a protocol to the United Nations Framework Convention on Climate Change (UNFCCC or FCCC), aimed at fighting global warming. The UNFCCC is an international environmental treaty with the goal of achieving `stabilization of greenhouse gas concentrations in the atmosphere at a level that would prevent dangerous anthropogenic interference with the climate system.`
	The Protocol was initially adopted on 11 December 1997 in Kyoto, Japan and entered into force on 16 February 2005. As of November 2009, 187 states have signed and ratified the protocol.
	Under the Protocol, 37 industrialized countries commit themselves to a reduction of four greenhouse gases (GHG) (carbon dioxide, methane, nitrous oxide, sulphur hexafluoride) and two groups of gases produced by them, and all member countries give general commitments.
Fair trade	Fair trade is an organized social movement and market-based approach that aims to help producers in developing countries obtain better trading conditions and promote sustainability. The movement advocates the payment of a higher price to producers as well as social and environmental standards. It focuses in particular on exports from developing countries to developed countries, most notably handicrafts, coffee, cocoa, sugar, tea, bananas, honey, cotton, wine, fresh fruit, chocolate and flowers.
Public Interest	The Public interest refers to the `common well-being` or `general welfare.` The Public interest is central to policy debates, politics, democracy and the nature of government itself. While nearly everyone claims that aiding the common well-being or general welfare is positive, there is little, if any, consensus on what exactly constitutes the Public interest.
	There are different views on how many members of the public must benefit from an action before it can be declared to be in the Public interest: at one extreme, an action has to benefit every single member of society in order to be truly in the Public interest; at the other extreme, any action can be in the Public interest as long as it benefits some of the population and harms none.
Race to the bottom	A Race to the bottom is a socio-economic concept that is argued to occur between countries as an outcome of regulatory competition. When competition becomes fierce between nations over a particular area of trade and production, countries are given increased incentive to dismantle currently existing regulatory standards.

Chapter 1. Introducing business ethics

A Race to the bottom may also occur within a country (such as between states or counties), but this occurs much less frequently because the federal government has recourse to enact legislation slowing or halting the race before its effects become too pervasive.

Business ethics

Business ethics is a form of applied ethics or professional ethics that examines ethical principles and moral or ethical problems that arise in a business environment. It applies to all aspects of business conduct and is relevant to the conduct of individuals and business organizations as a whole. Applied ethics is a field of ethics that deals with ethical questions in many fields such as medical, technical, legal and Business ethics.

Bribery

Bribery, a form of corruption, is an act implying money or gift given that alters the behavior of the recipient. Bribery constitutes a crime and is defined by Black`s Law Dictionary as the offering, giving, receiving, or soliciting of any item of value to influence the actions of an official or other person in charge of a public or legal duty. The bribe is the gift bestowed to influence the recipient`s conduct.

Sustainability

Sustainability is the capacity to endure. In ecology the word describes how biological systems remain diverse and productive over time. For humans it is the potential for long-term maintenance of well being, which in turn depends on the well being of the natural world and the responsible use of natural resources.

Environmental management

Environmental management is not, as the phrase could suggest, the management of the environment as such, but rather the management of interaction by the modern human societies with, and impact upon the environment. The three main issues that affect managers are those involving politics (networking), programs (projects), and resources (money, facilities, etc).. The need for Environmental management can be viewed from a variety of perspectives.

Sustainable development

Sustainable development is a pattern of resource use that aims to meet human needs while preserving the environment so that these needs can be met not only in the present, but also for future generations. The term was used by the Brundtland Commission which coined what has become the most often-quoted definition of Sustainable development as development that `meets the needs of the present without compromising the ability of future generations to meet their own needs.`

Sustainable development ties together concern for the carrying capacity of natural systems with the social challenges facing humanity. As early as the 1970s `sustainability` was employed to describe an economy `in equilibrium with basic ecological support systems.` Ecologists have pointed to The Limits to Growth, and presented the alternative of a `steady state economy` in order to address environmental concerns.

Chapter 1. Introducing business ethics

Triple bottom line	The Triple bottom line captures an expanded spectrum of values and criteria for measuring organizational (and societal) success: economic, ecological and social. With the ratification of the United Nations and ICLEI Triple bottom line standard for urban and community accounting in early 2007, this became the dominant approach to public sector full cost accounting. Similar UN standards apply to natural capital and human capital measurement to assist in measurements required by Triple bottom line, e.g. the ecoBudget standard for reporting ecological footprint.
Cartel	A Cartel is a formal (explicit) agreement among competing firms. It is a formal organization of producers and manufacturers that agree to fix prices, marketing, and production. Cartels usually occur in an oligopolistic industry, where there is a small number of sellers and usually involve homogeneous products.
Trade union	A Trade union or labor union is an organization of workers who have banded together to achieve common goals such as better working conditions. The Trade union, through its leadership, bargains with the employer on behalf of union members (rank and file members) and negotiates labour contracts (collective bargaining) with employers. This may include the negotiation of wages, work rules, complaint procedures, rules governing hiring, firing and promotion of workers, benefits, workplace safety and policies.
Stakeholder management	The importance of Stakeholder management is to support an organization in achieving its strategic objectives by interpreting and influencing both the external and internal environments and by creating positive relationships with stakeholders through the appropriate management of their expectations and agreed objectives. Stakeholder management is a process and control that must be planned and guided by underlying Principles.
Utilitarianism	Utilitarianism is the idea that the moral worth of an action is determined solely by its utility in providing happiness or pleasure as summed among all sentient beings. It is thus a form of consequentialism, meaning that the moral worth of an action is determined by its outcome. The most influential contributors to this ideology were Jeremy Bentham and John Stuart Mill.

Chapter 1. Introducing business ethics

Chapter 2. Framining business ethics

Corporate social responsibility	Corporate social responsibility also known as corporate responsibility, corporate citizenship, responsible business, sustainable responsible business (SRB), or corporate social performance, is a form of corporate self-regulation integrated into a business model. Ideally, Corporate social responsibility policy would function as a built-in, self-regulating mechanism whereby business would monitor and ensure its support to law, ethical standards, and international norms. Consequently, business would embrace responsibility for the impact of its activities on the environment, consumers, employees, communities, stakeholders and all other members of the public sphere.
Perpetual succession	In company law, Perpetual succession is the continuation of a corporation`s or other organization`s existence despite the death, bankruptcy, insanity, change in membership or an exit from the business of any owner or member, or any transfer of stock,etc,etc,etc.

Perpetual succession, along with a common seal, is one of the features defining a corporation`s legal existence as separate from those of its owners. |
Fiduciary	A Fiduciary duty is a legal or ethical relationship of confidence or trust regarding the management of money or property between two or more parties, most commonly a Fiduciary and a principal. One party, for example a corporate trust company or the trust department of a bank, holds a Fiduciary relation or acts in a Fiduciary capacity to another, such as one whose funds are entrusted to it for investment. In a Fiduciary relation one person, in a position of vulnerability, justifiably reposes confidence, good faith, reliance and trust in another whose aid, advice or protection is sought in some matter.
Business ethics	Business ethics is a form of applied ethics or professional ethics that examines ethical principles and moral or ethical problems that arise in a business environment. It applies to all aspects of business conduct and is relevant to the conduct of individuals and business organizations as a whole. Applied ethics is a field of ethics that deals with ethical questions in many fields such as medical, technical, legal and Business ethics.
Room	A Room, in architecture, is any distinguishable space within a structure. Usually, a Room is separated from other spaces or passageways by interior walls; moreover, it is separated from outdoor areas by an exterior wall, sometimes with a door. Historically the use of Rooms dates at least to early Minoan cultures about 2200 BC, where excavations on Santorini, Greece at Akrotiri reveal clearly defined Rooms within certain structures.

Chapter 2. Framining business ethics

Universal Declaration of Human Rights	The Universal Declaration of Human Rights is a declaration adopted by the United Nations General Assembly on 10 December 1948 at the Palais de Chaillot in Paris. The Declaration has been translated into at least 375 languages and dialects, making it the most widely translated document in the world. The Declaration arose directly from the experience of the Second World War and represents the first global expression of rights to which all human beings are entitled.
Cartel	A Cartel is a formal (explicit) agreement among competing firms. It is a formal organization of producers and manufacturers that agree to fix prices, marketing, and production. Cartels usually occur in an oligopolistic industry, where there is a small number of sellers and usually involve homogeneous products.
Kyoto Protocol	The Kyoto Protocol is a protocol to the United Nations Framework Convention on Climate Change (UNFCCC or FCCC), aimed at fighting global warming. The UNFCCC is an international environmental treaty with the goal of achieving `stabilization of greenhouse gas concentrations in the atmosphere at a level that would prevent dangerous anthropogenic interference with the climate system.` The Protocol was initially adopted on 11 December 1997 in Kyoto, Japan and entered into force on 16 February 2005. As of November 2009, 187 states have signed and ratified the protocol. Under the Protocol, 37 industrialized countries commit themselves to a reduction of four greenhouse gases (GHG) (carbon dioxide, methane, nitrous oxide, sulphur hexafluoride) and two groups of gases produced by them, and all member countries give general commitments.
Stakeholder management	The importance of Stakeholder management is to support an organization in achieving its strategic objectives by interpreting and influencing both the external and internal environments and by creating positive relationships with stakeholders through the appropriate management of their expectations and agreed objectives. Stakeholder management is a process and control that must be planned and guided by underlying Principles.
Global Reporting Initiative	

Chapter 2. Framining business ethics

The Global Reporting Initiative produces one of the world's most prevalent standards for sustainability reporting - also known as ecological footprint reporting, Environmental Social Governance (ESG) reporting, Triple Bottom Line (TBL) reporting, Corporate Social Responsibility (CSR) reporting. Sustainability reporting is a form of value reporting where an organization publicly communicates their economic, environmental, and social performance. Global Reporting Initiative seeks to make sustainability reporting by all organizations as routine as, and comparable to, financial reporting.

Millennium Development Goals	The Millennium Development Goals are eight international development goals that all 192 United Nations member states and at least 23 international organizations have agreed to achieve by the year 2015. They include reducing extreme poverty, reducing child mortality rates, fighting disease epidemics such as AIDS, and developing a global partnership for development.

In 2001, recognizing the need to assist impoverished nations more aggressively, UN member states adopted the targets. The Millennium Development Goalss aim to spur development by improving social and economic conditions in the world's poorest countries.

Environmental management	Environmental management is not, as the phrase could suggest, the management of the environment as such, but rather the management of interaction by the modern human societies with, and impact upon the environment. The three main issues that affect managers are those involving politics (networking), programs (projects), and resources (money, facilities, etc).. The need for Environmental management can be viewed from a variety of perspectives.

Public Interest	The Public interest refers to the `common well-being` or `general welfare.` The Public interest is central to policy debates, politics, democracy and the nature of government itself. While nearly everyone claims that aiding the common well-being or general welfare is positive, there is little, if any, consensus on what exactly constitutes the Public interest.

There are different views on how many members of the public must benefit from an action before it can be declared to be in the Public interest: at one extreme, an action has to benefit every single member of society in order to be truly in the Public interest; at the other extreme, any action can be in the Public interest as long as it benefits some of the population and harms none.

Chapter 2. Framining business ethics

Race to the bottom	A Race to the bottom is a socio-economic concept that is argued to occur between countries as an outcome of regulatory competition. When competition becomes fierce between nations over a particular area of trade and production, countries are given increased incentive to dismantle currently existing regulatory standards. A Race to the bottom may also occur within a country (such as between states or counties), but this occurs much less frequently because the federal government has recourse to enact legislation slowing or halting the race before its effects become too pervasive.
Sweatshop	Sweatshop is a working environment considered to be unacceptably difficult or dangerous -- particularly by industrialized nations with high standards of living. However Sweatshops may exist in any country. Sweatshop workers often work long hours for unusually low pay, regardless of laws mandating overtime pay or a minimum wage.
Intellectual property	Intellectual property is a term referring to a number of distinct types of creations of the mind for which property rights are recognised--and the corresponding fields of law. Under Intellectual property law, owners are granted certain exclusive rights to a variety of intangible assets, such as musical, literary, and artistic works; discoveries and inventions; and words, phrases, symbols, and designs. Common types of Intellectual property include copyrights, trademarks, patents, industrial design rights and trade secrets in some jurisdictions.

Chapter 3. Evaluating business ethics

Room	A Room, in architecture, is any distinguishable space within a structure. Usually, a Room is separated from other spaces or passageways by interior walls; moreover, it is separated from outdoor areas by an exterior wall, sometimes with a door. Historically the use of Rooms dates at least to early Minoan cultures about 2200 BC, where excavations on Santorini, Greece at Akrotiri reveal clearly defined Rooms within certain structures.
Universal Declaration of Human Rights	The Universal Declaration of Human Rights is a declaration adopted by the United Nations General Assembly on 10 December 1948 at the Palais de Chaillot in Paris. The Declaration has been translated into at least 375 languages and dialects, making it the most widely translated document in the world. The Declaration arose directly from the experience of the Second World War and represents the first global expression of rights to which all human beings are entitled.
Business ethics	Business ethics is a form of applied ethics or professional ethics that examines ethical principles and moral or ethical problems that arise in a business environment. It applies to all aspects of business conduct and is relevant to the conduct of individuals and business organizations as a whole. Applied ethics is a field of ethics that deals with ethical questions in many fields such as medical, technical, legal and Business ethics.
Consequentialism	Consequentialism refers to those moral theories which hold that the consequences of a particular action form the basis for any valid moral judgment about that action . Thus, from a consequentialist standpoint, a morally right action is one that produces a good outcome, or consequence. This view is often expressed as the aphorism `The ends justify the means`.
Utilitarianism	Utilitarianism is the idea that the moral worth of an action is determined solely by its utility in providing happiness or pleasure as summed among all sentient beings. It is thus a form of consequentialism, meaning that the moral worth of an action is determined by its outcome. The most influential contributors to this ideology were Jeremy Bentham and John Stuart Mill.
Child labour	Child labour refers to the employment of children at regular and sustained labour. This practice is considered exploitative by many international organizations and is illegal in many countries. Child labour was utilized to varying extents through most of history, but entered public dispute with the advent of universal schooling, with changes in working conditions during the industrial revolution, and with the emergence of the concepts of workers` and children`s rights.

Chapter 3. Evaluating business ethics

Corporate social responsibility	Corporate social responsibility also known as corporate responsibility, corporate citizenship, responsible business, sustainable responsible business (SRB), or corporate social performance, is a form of corporate self-regulation integrated into a business model. Ideally, Corporate social responsibility policy would function as a built-in, self-regulating mechanism whereby business would monitor and ensure its support to law, ethical standards, and international norms. Consequently, business would embrace responsibility for the impact of its activities on the environment, consumers, employees, communities, stakeholders and all other members of the public sphere.
Cost-benefit analysis	Cost-benefit analysis is a term that refers both to: · helping to appraise, or assess, the case for a project, programme or policy proposal; · an approach to making economic decisions of any kind Under both definitions the process involves, whether explicitly or implicitly, weighing the total expected costs against the total expected benefits of one or more actions in order to choose the best or most profitable option. The formal process is often referred to as either Cost benefit analysis (Cost-benefit analysis) or BCA (Benefit-Cost Analysis). Benefits and costs are often expressed in money terms, and are adjusted for the time value of money, so that all flows of benefits and flows of project costs over time are expressed on a common basis in terms of their `present value.` Closely related, but slightly different, formal techniques include cost-effectiveness analysis, economic impact analysis, fiscal impact analysis and Social Return on Investment (SROI) analysis.
Land rights	Land rights are those property rights that pertain to real estate land. Because land is a limited resource and property rights include the right to exclude others, Land rights are a form of monopoly. Those without Land rights must enter into land use agreements, as they must reside somewhere.

Chapter 3. Evaluating business ethics

Procedural justice	Procedural justice refers to the idea of fairness in the processes that resolve disputes and allocate resources. One aspect of Procedural justice is related to discussions of the administration of justice and legal proceedings. This sense of Procedural justice is connected to due process (U.S)., fundamental justice (Canada), procedural fairness (Australia) and natural justice (other Common law jurisdictions), but the idea of Procedural justice can also be applied to nonlegal contexts in which some process is employed to resolve conflict or divide benefits or burdens.
Entitlement theory	Entitlement theory is a theory of distributive justice and private property created by Robert Nozick in his book Anarchy, State, and Utopia. The theory is Nozick's attempt to describe `justice in holdings` - or what can be said about and done with the property people own when viewed from a principle of justice.

Nozick's Entitlement theory comprises 3 main principles:

· A principle of justice in acquisition - This principle deals with the initial acquisition of holdings. It is an account of how people first come to own common property, what types of things can be held, and so forth.

· A principle of justice in transfer - This principle explains how one person can acquire holdings from another, including voluntary exchange and gifts.

· A principle of rectification of injustice - how to deal with holdings that are unjustly acquired or transferred, whether and how much victims can be compensated, how to deal with long past transgressions or injustices done by a government, and so on.
Nozick believes that if the world were wholly just, only the first two principles would be needed, as `the following inductive definition would exhaustively cover the subject of justice in holdings`:

· A person who acquires a holding in accordance with the principle of justice in acquisition is entitled to that holding

· A person who acquires a holding in accordance with the principle of justice in transfer, from someone else entitled to the holding, is entitled to the holding

· No one is entitled to a holding except by (repeated) applications of 1 and 2.

Thus, Entitlement theory would imply `a distribution is just if everyone is entitled to the holdings they possess under the distribution` . |

Chapter 3. Evaluating business ethics

Sweatshop	Sweatshop is a working environment considered to be unacceptably difficult or dangerous -- particularly by industrialized nations with high standards of living. However Sweatshops may exist in any country. Sweatshop workers often work long hours for unusually low pay, regardless of laws mandating overtime pay or a minimum wage.
Discourse ethics	Discourse ethics refers to a type of argument that attempts to establish normative or ethical truths by examining the presuppositions of discourse.
	German philosophers Jürgen Habermas and Karl-Otto Apel are probably properly considered as the originators of modern Discourse ethics. Habermas`s Discourse ethics is his attempt to explain the implications of communicative rationality in the sphere of moral insight and normative validity.
Virtue ethics	Virtue ethics is an approach to ethics that emphasizes the character of the moral agent, rather than rules or consequences, as the key element of ethical thinking. This contrasts with consequentialism, which holds that the consequences of a particular act form the basis for any valid moral judgment about that action, and deontology, which derives rightness or wrongness from the character of the act itself rather than the outcomes. The difference between these three approaches to morality tends to lie more in the way moral dilemmas are approached than in the moral conclusions reached.
Affirmative action	Affirmative action refers to policies that take factors including `race, color, religion, sex or national origin` into consideration in order to benefit an underrepresented group, usually as a means to counter the effects of a history of discrimination. The focus of such policies ranges from employment and education to public contracting and health programs. `Affirmative action` is action taken to increase the representation of women and minorities in areas of employment, education, and business from which they have been historically excluded.
Trade union	A Trade union or labor union is an organization of workers who have banded together to achieve common goals such as better working conditions. The Trade union, through its leadership, bargains with the employer on behalf of union members (rank and file members) and negotiates labour contracts (collective bargaining) with employers. This may include the negotiation of wages, work rules, complaint procedures, rules governing hiring, firing and promotion of workers, benefits, workplace safety and policies.

Chapter 3. Evaluating business ethics

Bribery	Bribery, a form of corruption, is an act implying money or gift given that alters the behavior of the recipient. Bribery constitutes a crime and is defined by Black`s Law Dictionary as the offering, giving, receiving, or soliciting of any item of value to influence the actions of an official or other person in charge of a public or legal duty. The bribe is the gift bestowed to influence the recipient`s conduct.

Chapter 4. Making decisions in business ethics

Room	A Room, in architecture, is any distinguishable space within a structure. Usually, a Room is separated from other spaces or passageways by interior walls; moreover, it is separated from outdoor areas by an exterior wall, sometimes with a door. Historically the use of Rooms dates at least to early Minoan cultures about 2200 BC, where excavations on Santorini, Greece at Akrotiri reveal clearly defined Rooms within certain structures.
Bribery	Bribery, a form of corruption, is an act implying money or gift given that alters the behavior of the recipient. Bribery constitutes a crime and is defined by Black's Law Dictionary as the offering, giving, receiving, or soliciting of any item of value to influence the actions of an official or other person in charge of a public or legal duty. The bribe is the gift bestowed to influence the recipient's conduct.
Consequentialism	Consequentialism refers to those moral theories which hold that the consequences of a particular action form the basis for any valid moral judgment about that action . Thus, from a consequentialist standpoint, a morally right action is one that produces a good outcome, or consequence. This view is often expressed as the aphorism `The ends justify the means`.
Cost-benefit analysis	Cost-benefit analysis is a term that refers both to: · helping to appraise, or assess, the case for a project, programme or policy proposal; · an approach to making economic decisions of any kind Under both definitions the process involves, whether explicitly or implicitly, weighing the total expected costs against the total expected benefits of one or more actions in order to choose the best or most profitable option. The formal process is often referred to as either Cost benefit analysis (Cost-benefit analysis) or BCA (Benefit-Cost Analysis). Benefits and costs are often expressed in money terms, and are adjusted for the time value of money, so that all flows of benefits and flows of project costs over time are expressed on a common basis in terms of their `present value.` Closely related, but slightly different, formal techniques include cost-effectiveness analysis, economic impact analysis, fiscal impact analysis and Social Return on Investment (SROI) analysis.

Chapter 4. Making decisions in business ethics

Organizational culture	Organizational culture is an idea in the field of Organizational studies and management which describes the psychology, attitudes, experiences, beliefs and values (personal and cultural values) of an organization. It has been defined as `the specific collection of values and norms that are shared by people and groups in an organization and that control the way they interact with each other and with stakeholders outside the organization.`
	This definition continues to explain organizational values, also known as `beliefs and ideas about what kinds of goals members of an organization should pursue and ideas about the appropriate kinds or standards of behavior organizational members should use to achieve these goals. From organizational values develop organizational norms, guidelines, or expectations that prescribe appropriate kinds of behavior by employees in particular situations and control the behavior of organizational members towards one another.`
	Organizational culture and corporate culture are often used interchangeably but it is a mistake to state that they are different concepts.
Millennium Development Goals	The Millennium Development Goals are eight international development goals that all 192 United Nations member states and at least 23 international organizations have agreed to achieve by the year 2015. They include reducing extreme poverty, reducing child mortality rates, fighting disease epidemics such as AIDS, and developing a global partnership for development.
	In 2001, recognizing the need to assist impoverished nations more aggressively, UN member states adopted the targets. The Millennium Development Goalss aim to spur development by improving social and economic conditions in the world`s poorest countries.
Universal Declaration of Human Rights	The Universal Declaration of Human Rights is a declaration adopted by the United Nations General Assembly on 10 December 1948 at the Palais de Chaillot in Paris. The Declaration has been translated into at least 375 languages and dialects, making it the most widely translated document in the world. The Declaration arose directly from the experience of the Second World War and represents the first global expression of rights to which all human beings are entitled.
Locus of control	Locus of control in social psychology refers to the extent to which individuals believe that they can control events that affect them. Understanding of the concept was developed by Julian B. Rotter in 1954, and has since become an important aspect of personality studies.

Chapter 4. Making decisions in business ethics

	Individuals with a high internal Locus of control believe that events result primarily from their own behavior and actions.
Business ethics	Business ethics is a form of applied ethics or professional ethics that examines ethical principles and moral or ethical problems that arise in a business environment. It applies to all aspects of business conduct and is relevant to the conduct of individuals and business organizations as a whole. Applied ethics is a field of ethics that deals with ethical questions in many fields such as medical, technical, legal and Business ethics.
Public Interest	The Public interest refers to the `common well-being` or `general welfare.` The Public interest is central to policy debates, politics, democracy and the nature of government itself. While nearly everyone claims that aiding the common well-being or general welfare is positive, there is little, if any, consensus on what exactly constitutes the Public interest.
	There are different views on how many members of the public must benefit from an action before it can be declared to be in the Public interest: at one extreme, an action has to benefit every single member of society in order to be truly in the Public interest; at the other extreme, any action can be in the Public interest as long as it benefits some of the population and harms none.
Stanford Prison Experiment	The Stanford prison experiment was a study of the psychological effects of becoming a prisoner or prison guard. The experiment was conducted in 1971 by a team of researchers led by Psychology Professor Dr. Philip Zimbardo, Ph.D., at Stanford University. Twenty-four undergraduates were selected out of over 75 to play the roles of both guards and prisoners and live in a mock prison in the basement of the Stanford psychology building.
Kyoto Protocol	The Kyoto Protocol is a protocol to the United Nations Framework Convention on Climate Change (UNFCCC or FCCC), aimed at fighting global warming. The UNFCCC is an international environmental treaty with the goal of achieving `stabilization of greenhouse gas concentrations in the atmosphere at a level that would prevent dangerous anthropogenic interference with the climate system.`
	The Protocol was initially adopted on 11 December 1997 in Kyoto, Japan and entered into force on 16 February 2005. As of November 2009, 187 states have signed and ratified the protocol.

Under the Protocol, 37 industrialized countries commit themselves to a reduction of four greenhouse gases (GHG) (carbon dioxide, methane, nitrous oxide, sulphur hexafluoride) and two groups of gases produced by them, and all member countries give general commitments.

Corporate social responsibility

Corporate social responsibility also known as corporate responsibility, corporate citizenship, responsible business, sustainable responsible business (SRB), or corporate social performance, is a form of corporate self-regulation integrated into a business model. Ideally, Corporate social responsibility policy would function as a built-in, self-regulating mechanism whereby business would monitor and ensure its support to law, ethical standards, and international norms. Consequently, business would embrace responsibility for the impact of its activities on the environment, consumers, employees, communities, stakeholders and all other members of the public sphere.

Chapter 5. managing business ethics

Business ethics	Business ethics is a form of applied ethics or professional ethics that examines ethical principles and moral or ethical problems that arise in a business environment. It applies to all aspects of business conduct and is relevant to the conduct of individuals and business organizations as a whole. Applied ethics is a field of ethics that deals with ethical questions in many fields such as medical, technical, legal and Business ethics.
Millennium Development Goals	The Millennium Development Goals are eight international development goals that all 192 United Nations member states and at least 23 international organizations have agreed to achieve by the year 2015. They include reducing extreme poverty, reducing child mortality rates, fighting disease epidemics such as AIDS, and developing a global partnership for development. In 2001, recognizing the need to assist impoverished nations more aggressively, UN member states adopted the targets. The Millennium Development Goalss aim to spur development by improving social and economic conditions in the world`s poorest countries.
Universal Declaration of Human Rights	The Universal Declaration of Human Rights is a declaration adopted by the United Nations General Assembly on 10 December 1948 at the Palais de Chaillot in Paris. The Declaration has been translated into at least 375 languages and dialects, making it the most widely translated document in the world. The Declaration arose directly from the experience of the Second World War and represents the first global expression of rights to which all human beings are entitled.
Foreign Corrupt Practices Act	The Foreign Corrupt Practices Act of 1977 (15 U.S.C. Â§Â§ 78dd-1, et seq). is a United States federal law known primarily for two of its main provisions, one that addresses accounting transparency requirements under the Securities Exchange Act of 1934 and another concerning bribery of foreign officials. The anti-bribery provisions of the Foreign Corrupt Practices Act prohibit: Issuers, domestic concerns, and any person from making use of interstate commerce corruptly, in furtherance of an offer or payment of anything of value to a foreign official, foreign political party, or candidate for political office, for the purpose of influencing any act of that foreign official in violation of the duty of that official, or to secure any improper advantage in order to obtain or retain business.

Chapter 5. managing business ethics

Bribery	Bribery, a form of corruption, is an act implying money or gift given that alters the behavior of the recipient. Bribery constitutes a crime and is defined by Black`s Law Dictionary as the offering, giving, receiving, or soliciting of any item of value to influence the actions of an official or other person in charge of a public or legal duty. The bribe is the gift bestowed to influence the recipient`s conduct.
Global Reporting Initiative	The Global Reporting Initiative produces one of the world`s most prevalent standards for sustainability reporting - also known as ecological footprint reporting, Environmental Social Governance (ESG) reporting, Triple Bottom Line (TBL) reporting, Corporate Social Responsibility (CSR) reporting. Sustainability reporting is a form of value reporting where an organization publicly communicates their economic, environmental, and social performance. Global Reporting Initiative seeks to make sustainability reporting by all organizations as routine as, and comparable to, financial reporting.
Organization	An Organization is a social arrangement which pursues collective goals, controls its own performance, and has a boundary separating it from its environment. The word itself is derived from the Greek word organon, itself derived from the better-known word ergon. In the social sciences, Organizations are the object of analysis for a number of disciplines, such as sociology, economics, political science, psychology, management, and Organizational communication.
Social accounting	Social accounting is the process of communicating the social and environmental effects of organizations` economic actions to particular interest groups within society and to society at large. Social accounting is commonly used in the context of business, or corporate social responsibility (CSR), although any organisation, including NGOs, charities, and government agencies may engage in Social accounting. Social accounting emphasises the notion of corporate accountability.

Chapter 5. managing business ethics

Stakeholder management	The importance of Stakeholder management is to support an organization in achieving its strategic objectives by interpreting and influencing both the external and internal environments and by creating positive relationships with stakeholders through the appropriate management of their expectations and agreed objectives. Stakeholder management is a process and control that must be planned and guided by underlying Principles.
Room	A Room, in architecture, is any distinguishable space within a structure. Usually, a Room is separated from other spaces or passageways by interior walls; moreover, it is separated from outdoor areas by an exterior wall, sometimes with a door. Historically the use of Rooms dates at least to early Minoan cultures about 2200 BC, where excavations on Santorini, Greece at Akrotiri reveal clearly defined Rooms within certain structures.
Environmental management	Environmental management is not, as the phrase could suggest, the management of the environment as such, but rather the management of interaction by the modern human societies with, and impact upon the environment. The three main issues that affect managers are those involving politics (networking), programs (projects), and resources (money, facilities, etc).. The need for Environmental management can be viewed from a variety of perspectives.
Industrial espionage	Industrial espionage, economic espionage or corporate espionage is espionage conducted for commercial purposes instead of purely national security purposes. Economic espionage is conducted or orchestrated by governments and is international in scope, while industrial or corporate espionage is more often national and occurs between companies or corporations. `Competitive intelligence` describes the legal and ethical activity of systematically gathering, analyzing and managing information on industrial competitors.
Trade union	A Trade union or labor union is an organization of workers who have banded together to achieve common goals such as better working conditions. The Trade union, through its leadership, bargains with the employer on behalf of union members (rank and file members) and negotiates labour contracts (collective bargaining) with employers. This may include the negotiation of wages, work rules, complaint procedures, rules governing hiring, firing and promotion of workers, benefits, workplace safety and policies.
Sustainability	Sustainability is the capacity to endure. In ecology the word describes how biological systems remain diverse and productive over time. For humans it is the potential for long-term maintenance of well being, which in turn depends on the well being of the natural world and the responsible use of natural resources.

Chapter 5. managing business ethics

Triple bottom line	The Triple bottom line captures an expanded spectrum of values and criteria for measuring organizational (and societal) success: economic, ecological and social. With the ratification of the United Nations and ICLEI Triple bottom line standard for urban and community accounting in early 2007, this became the dominant approach to public sector full cost accounting. Similar UN standards apply to natural capital and human capital measurement to assist in measurements required by Triple bottom line, e.g. the ecoBudget standard for reporting ecological footprint.
Kyoto Protocol	The Kyoto Protocol is a protocol to the United Nations Framework Convention on Climate Change (UNFCCC or FCCC), aimed at fighting global warming. The UNFCCC is an international environmental treaty with the goal of achieving `stabilization of greenhouse gas concentrations in the atmosphere at a level that would prevent dangerous anthropogenic interference with the climate system.`
	The Protocol was initially adopted on 11 December 1997 in Kyoto, Japan and entered into force on 16 February 2005. As of November 2009, 187 states have signed and ratified the protocol.
	Under the Protocol, 37 industrialized countries commit themselves to a reduction of four greenhouse gases (GHG) (carbon dioxide, methane, nitrous oxide, sulphur hexafluoride) and two groups of gases produced by them, and all member countries give general commitments.
Discourse ethics	Discourse ethics refers to a type of argument that attempts to establish normative or ethical truths by examining the presuppositions of discourse.
	German philosophers Jürgen Habermas and Karl-Otto Apel are probably properly considered as the originators of modern Discourse ethics. Habermas`s Discourse ethics is his attempt to explain the implications of communicative rationality in the sphere of moral insight and normative validity.
Cost-benefit analysis	Cost-benefit analysis is a term that refers both to:
	· helping to appraise, or assess, the case for a project, programme or policy proposal;
	· an approach to making economic decisions of any kind

Under both definitions the process involves, whether explicitly or implicitly, weighing the total expected costs against the total expected benefits of one or more actions in order to choose the best or most profitable option. The formal process is often referred to as either Cost benefit analysis (Cost-benefit analysis) or BCA (Benefit-Cost Analysis).

Benefits and costs are often expressed in money terms, and are adjusted for the time value of money, so that all flows of benefits and flows of project costs over time are expressed on a common basis in terms of their `present value.` Closely related, but slightly different, formal techniques include cost-effectiveness analysis, economic impact analysis, fiscal impact analysis and Social Return on Investment (SROI) analysis.

Sustainable development

Sustainable development is a pattern of resource use that aims to meet human needs while preserving the environment so that these needs can be met not only in the present, but also for future generations. The term was used by the Brundtland Commission which coined what has become the most often-quoted definition of Sustainable development as development that `meets the needs of the present without compromising the ability of future generations to meet their own needs.`

Sustainable development ties together concern for the carrying capacity of natural systems with the social challenges facing humanity. As early as the 1970s `sustainability` was employed to describe an economy `in equilibrium with basic ecological support systems.` Ecologists have pointed to The Limits to Growth, and presented the alternative of a `steady state economy` in order to address environmental concerns.

Chapter 6. shareholders and business ethics

Millennium Development Goals	The Millennium Development Goals are eight international development goals that all 192 United Nations member states and at least 23 international organizations have agreed to achieve by the year 2015. They include reducing extreme poverty, reducing child mortality rates, fighting disease epidemics such as AIDS, and developing a global partnership for development. In 2001, recognizing the need to assist impoverished nations more aggressively, UN member states adopted the targets. The Millennium Development Goalss aim to spur development by improving social and economic conditions in the world`s poorest countries.
Insider trading	Insider trading is the trading of a corporation`s stock or other securities (e.g. bonds or stock options) by individuals with potential access to non-public information about the company. In most countries, trading by corporate insiders such as officers, key employees, directors, and large shareholders may be legal, if this trading is done in a way that does not take advantage of non-public information. However, the term is frequently used to refer to a practice in which an insider or a related party trades based on material non-public information obtained during the performance of the insider`s duties at the corporation, or otherwise in breach of a fiduciary or other relationship of trust and confidence or where the non-public information was misappropriated from the company.
Money laundering	In US law, Money laundering is the practice of engaging in financial transactions to conceal the identity, source, or destination of illegally gained money. In UK law the common law definition is wider: `taking any action with property of any form which is either wholly or in part the proceeds of a crime that will disguise the fact that that property is the proceeds of a crime or obscure the beneficial ownership of said property.` In the past, the term Money laundering was applied only to financial transactions related to organized crime. Today its definition is often expanded by government and international regulators such as the US Office of the Comptroller of the Currency to mean any financial transaction which generates an asset or a value as the result of an illegal act, which may involve actions such as tax evasion or false accounting.
Locus of control	Locus of control in social psychology refers to the extent to which individuals believe that they can control events that affect them. Understanding of the concept was developed by Julian B. Rotter in 1954, and has since become an important aspect of personality studies.

Chapter 6. shareholders and business ethics

	Individuals with a high internal Locus of control believe that events result primarily from their own behavior and actions.
Sustainability	Sustainability is the capacity to endure. In ecology the word describes how biological systems remain diverse and productive over time. For humans it is the potential for long-term maintenance of well being, which in turn depends on the well being of the natural world and the responsible use of natural resources.
Kyoto Protocol	The Kyoto Protocol is a protocol to the United Nations Framework Convention on Climate Change (UNFCCC or FCCC), aimed at fighting global warming. The UNFCCC is an international environmental treaty with the goal of achieving `stabilization of greenhouse gas concentrations in the atmosphere at a level that would prevent dangerous anthropogenic interference with the climate system.`
	The Protocol was initially adopted on 11 December 1997 in Kyoto, Japan and entered into force on 16 February 2005. As of November 2009, 187 states have signed and ratified the protocol.
	Under the Protocol, 37 industrialized countries commit themselves to a reduction of four greenhouse gases (GHG) (carbon dioxide, methane, nitrous oxide, sulphur hexafluoride) and two groups of gases produced by them, and all member countries give general commitments.
Mergers and acquisitions	The phrase Mergers and acquisitions refers to the aspect of corporate strategy, corporate finance and management dealing with the buying, selling and combining of different companies that can aid, finance, or help a growing company in a given industry grow rapidly without having to create another business entity.
	An acquisition, also known as a takeover or a buyout, is the buying of one company (the `target`) by another. Consolidation is when two companies combine together to form a new company alltogether.
Trade union	A Trade union or labor union is an organization of workers who have banded together to achieve common goals such as better working conditions. The Trade union, through its leadership, bargains with the employer on behalf of union members (rank and file members) and negotiates labour contracts (collective bargaining) with employers. This may include the negotiation of wages, work rules, complaint procedures, rules governing hiring, firing and promotion of workers, benefits, workplace safety and policies.

Chapter 6. shareholders and business ethics

Performance-related pay	Performance-related pay is money paid to someone relating to how well he or she works at the workplace. Car salesmen, production line workers, for example, may be paid in this way, or through commission. Business theorist Frederick Winslow Taylor was a great supporter of this method of payment, which is often referred to as Performance related pay. He believed money was the main incentive for increased productivity and introducing the widely used concept of `piece work`.
Room	A Room, in architecture, is any distinguishable space within a structure. Usually, a Room is separated from other spaces or passageways by interior walls; moreover, it is separated from outdoor areas by an exterior wall, sometimes with a door. Historically the use of Rooms dates at least to early Minoan cultures about 2200 BC, where excavations on Santorini, Greece at Akrotiri reveal clearly defined Rooms within certain structures.
Fiduciary	A Fiduciary duty is a legal or ethical relationship of confidence or trust regarding the management of money or property between two or more parties, most commonly a Fiduciary and a principal. One party, for example a corporate trust company or the trust department of a bank, holds a Fiduciary relation or acts in a Fiduciary capacity to another, such as one whose funds are entrusted to it for investment. In a Fiduciary relation one person, in a position of vulnerability, justifiably reposes confidence, good faith, reliance and trust in another whose aid, advice or protection is sought in some matter.
Creative accounting	Creative accounting and earnings management are euphemisms referring to accounting practices that may follow the letter of the rules of standard accounting practices, but certainly deviate from the spirit of those rules. They are characterized by excessive complication and the use of novel ways of characterizing income, assets, or liabilities and the intent to influence readers towards the interpretations desired by the authors. The terms `innovative` or `aggressive` are also sometimes used.
Social accounting	Social accounting is the process of communicating the social and environmental effects of organizations` economic actions to particular interest groups within society and to society at large. Social accounting is commonly used in the context of business, or corporate social responsibility (CSR), although any organisation, including NGOs, charities, and government agencies may engage in Social accounting.

Chapter 6. shareholders and business ethics

Social accounting emphasises the notion of corporate accountability.

Bribery	Bribery, a form of corruption, is an act implying money or gift given that alters the behavior of the recipient. Bribery constitutes a crime and is defined by Black`s Law Dictionary as the offering, giving, receiving, or soliciting of any item of value to influence the actions of an official or other person in charge of a public or legal duty. The bribe is the gift bestowed to influence the recipient`s conduct.
Environmental management	Environmental management is not, as the phrase could suggest, the management of the environment as such, but rather the management of interaction by the modern human societies with, and impact upon the environment. The three main issues that affect managers are those involving politics (networking), programs (projects), and resources (money, facilities, etc).. The need for Environmental management can be viewed from a variety of perspectives.
Triple bottom line	The Triple bottom line captures an expanded spectrum of values and criteria for measuring organizational (and societal) success: economic, ecological and social. With the ratification of the United Nations and ICLEI Triple bottom line standard for urban and community accounting in early 2007, this became the dominant approach to public sector full cost accounting. Similar UN standards apply to natural capital and human capital measurement to assist in measurements required by Triple bottom line, e.g. the ecoBudget standard for reporting ecological footprint.
Alliance	An Alliance is an agreement or friendship between two or more parties, made in order to advance common goals and to secure common interests.

.

Chapter 7. Employees and business ethics

Millennium Development Goals	The Millennium Development Goals are eight international development goals that all 192 United Nations member states and at least 23 international organizations have agreed to achieve by the year 2015. They include reducing extreme poverty, reducing child mortality rates, fighting disease epidemics such as AIDS, and developing a global partnership for development. In 2001, recognizing the need to assist impoverished nations more aggressively, UN member states adopted the targets. The Millennium Development Goalss aim to spur development by improving social and economic conditions in the world`s poorest countries.
Moral hazard	Moral hazard occurs when a party insulated from risk may behave differently than it would behave if it were fully exposed to the risk. Moral hazard is a special case of information asymmetry, a situation in which one party in a transaction has more information than another. The party that is insulated from risk generally has more information about its actions and intentions than the party paying for the negative consequences of the risk.
Corporate social responsibility	Corporate social responsibility also known as corporate responsibility, corporate citizenship, responsible business, sustainable responsible business (SRB), or corporate social performance, is a form of corporate self-regulation integrated into a business model. Ideally, Corporate social responsibility policy would function as a built-in, self-regulating mechanism whereby business would monitor and ensure its support to law, ethical standards, and international norms. Consequently, business would embrace responsibility for the impact of its activities on the environment, consumers, employees, communities, stakeholders and all other members of the public sphere.
Trade union	A Trade union or labor union is an organization of workers who have banded together to achieve common goals such as better working conditions. The Trade union, through its leadership, bargains with the employer on behalf of union members (rank and file members) and negotiates labour contracts (collective bargaining) with employers. This may include the negotiation of wages, work rules, complaint procedures, rules governing hiring, firing and promotion of workers, benefits, workplace safety and policies.

Chapter 7. Employees and business ethics

Affirmative action	Affirmative action refers to policies that take factors including `race, color, religion, sex or national origin` into consideration in order to benefit an underrepresented group, usually as a means to counter the effects of a history of discrimination. The focus of such policies ranges from employment and education to public contracting and health programs. `Affirmative action` is action taken to increase the representation of women and minorities in areas of employment, education, and business from which they have been historically excluded.
Bribery	Bribery, a form of corruption, is an act implying money or gift given that alters the behavior of the recipient. Bribery constitutes a crime and is defined by Black`s Law Dictionary as the offering, giving, receiving, or soliciting of any item of value to influence the actions of an official or other person in charge of a public or legal duty. The bribe is the gift bestowed to influence the recipient`s conduct.
Minimum wage	A Minimum wage is the lowest hourly, daily or monthly wage that employers may legally pay to employees or workers. Equivalently, it is the lowest wage at which workers may sell their labor. Although Minimum wage laws are in effect in a great many jurisdictions, there are differences of opinion about the benefits and drawbacks of a Minimum wage.
Reverse discrimination	Reverse discrimination is a specific form of discrimination against members of a dominant or majority group, or in favor of members of a minority or historically disadvantaged group. Groups may be defined in terms of race, gender, ethnicity, or other factors. This discrimination may seek to redress social inequalities where minority groups have been denied access to the same privileges of the majority group.
Sexual harassment	Sexual harassment is intimidation, bullying or coercion of a sexual nature, or the unwelcome or inappropriate promise of rewards in exchange for sexual favors. In some contexts or circumstances, Sexual harassment may be illegal. It includes a range of behavior from seemingly mild transgressions and annoyances to actual sexual abuse or sexual assault.
Work-life balance	Work-life balance is a broad concept including proper prioritizing between `work` (career and ambition) on one hand and `life` (pleasure, leisure, family and spiritual development) on the other. Related, though broader, terms include `lifestyle balance` and `life balance`. The expression was first used in the late 1970s to describe the balance between an individual`s work and personal life.

Chapter 7. Employees and business ethics

Procedural justice	Procedural justice refers to the idea of fairness in the processes that resolve disputes and allocate resources. One aspect of Procedural justice is related to discussions of the administration of justice and legal proceedings. This sense of Procedural justice is connected to due process (U.S)., fundamental justice (Canada), procedural fairness (Australia) and natural justice (other Common law jurisdictions), but the idea of Procedural justice can also be applied to nonlegal contexts in which some process is employed to resolve conflict or divide benefits or burdens.
Kyoto Protocol	The Kyoto Protocol is a protocol to the United Nations Framework Convention on Climate Change (UNFCCC or FCCC), aimed at fighting global warming. The UNFCCC is an international environmental treaty with the goal of achieving `stabilization of greenhouse gas concentrations in the atmosphere at a level that would prevent dangerous anthropogenic interference with the climate system.` The Protocol was initially adopted on 11 December 1997 in Kyoto, Japan and entered into force on 16 February 2005. As of November 2009, 187 states have signed and ratified the protocol. Under the Protocol, 37 industrialized countries commit themselves to a reduction of four greenhouse gases (GHG) (carbon dioxide, methane, nitrous oxide, sulphur hexafluoride) and two groups of gases produced by them, and all member countries give general commitments.
Universal Declaration of Human Rights	The Universal Declaration of Human Rights is a declaration adopted by the United Nations General Assembly on 10 December 1948 at the Palais de Chaillot in Paris. The Declaration has been translated into at least 375 languages and dialects, making it the most widely translated document in the world. The Declaration arose directly from the experience of the Second World War and represents the first global expression of rights to which all human beings are entitled.
Utilitarianism	Utilitarianism is the idea that the moral worth of an action is determined solely by its utility in providing happiness or pleasure as summed among all sentient beings. It is thus a form of consequentialism, meaning that the moral worth of an action is determined by its outcome. The most influential contributors to this ideology were Jeremy Bentham and John Stuart Mill.
Mergers and acquisitions	The phrase Mergers and acquisitions refers to the aspect of corporate strategy, corporate finance and management dealing with the buying, selling and combining of different companies that can aid, finance, or help a growing company in a given industry grow rapidly without having to create another business entity.

Chapter 7. Employees and business ethics

	An acquisition, also known as a takeover or a buyout, is the buying of one company (the `target`) by another. Consolidation is when two companies combine together to form a new company alltogether.
Precautionary principle	The Precautionary principle states that if an action or policy has a suspected risk of causing harm to the public or to the environment, in the absence of scientific consensus that the action or policy is harmful, the burden of proof that it is not harmful falls on those taking the action. This principle allows policy makers to make discretionary decisions in situations where there is the possibility of harm from taking a particular course or making a certain decision when extensive scientific knowledge on the matter is lacking. The principle implies that there is a social responsibility to protect the public from exposure to harm, when scientific investigation has found a plausible risk.
Room	A Room, in architecture, is any distinguishable space within a structure. Usually, a Room is separated from other spaces or passageways by interior walls; moreover, it is separated from outdoor areas by an exterior wall, sometimes with a door. Historically the use of Rooms dates at least to early Minoan cultures about 2200 BC, where excavations on Santorini, Greece at Akrotiri reveal clearly defined Rooms within certain structures.
Performance-related pay	Performance-related pay is money paid to someone relating to how well he or she works at the workplace. Car salesmen, production line workers, for example, may be paid in this way, or through commission. Business theorist Frederick Winslow Taylor was a great supporter of this method of payment, which is often referred to as Performance related pay. He believed money was the main incentive for increased productivity and introducing the widely used concept of `piece work`.
Public Interest	The Public interest refers to the `common well-being` or `general welfare.` The Public interest is central to policy debates, politics, democracy and the nature of government itself. While nearly everyone claims that aiding the common well-being or general welfare is positive, there is little, if any, consensus on what exactly constitutes the Public interest.

Chapter 7. Employees and business ethics

Chapter 7. Employees and business ethics

There are different views on how many members of the public must benefit from an action before it can be declared to be in the Public interest: at one extreme, an action has to benefit every single member of society in order to be truly in the Public interest; at the other extreme, any action can be in the Public interest as long as it benefits some of the population and harms none.

Creative accounting

Creative accounting and earnings management are euphemisms referring to accounting practices that may follow the letter of the rules of standard accounting practices, but certainly deviate from the spirit of those rules. They are characterized by excessive complication and the use of novel ways of characterizing income, assets, or liabilities and the intent to influence readers towards the interpretations desired by the authors. The terms `innovative` or `aggressive` are also sometimes used.

Business ethics

Business ethics is a form of applied ethics or professional ethics that examines ethical principles and moral or ethical problems that arise in a business environment. It applies to all aspects of business conduct and is relevant to the conduct of individuals and business organizations as a whole. Applied ethics is a field of ethics that deals with ethical questions in many fields such as medical, technical, legal and Business ethics.

Race to the bottom

A Race to the bottom is a socio-economic concept that is argued to occur between countries as an outcome of regulatory competition. When competition becomes fierce between nations over a particular area of trade and production, countries are given increased incentive to dismantle currently existing regulatory standards.

A Race to the bottom may also occur within a country (such as between states or counties), but this occurs much less frequently because the federal government has recourse to enact legislation slowing or halting the race before its effects become too pervasive.

Sustainability

Sustainability is the capacity to endure. In ecology the word describes how biological systems remain diverse and productive over time. For humans it is the potential for long-term maintenance of well being, which in turn depends on the well being of the natural world and the responsible use of natural resources.

Fordism

Fordism refers to various social theories about production and related socio-economic phenomena. It has varying but related meanings in different fields, as well as for Marxist and non-Marxist scholars. The essential meaning is that the worker must be paid higher wages in order to afford the products that the industrialist himself produces, causing an economy that runs full-circle.

Chapter 7. Employees and business ethics

| Working Time | Working time is the period of time that an individual spends at paid occupational labor. Unpaid labors such as personal housework are not considered part of the working week. Many countries regulate the work week by law, such as stipulating minimum daily rest periods, annual holidays and a maximum number of working hours per week. |

Chapter 8. Consumers and business ethics

Room	A Room, in architecture, is any distinguishable space within a structure. Usually, a Room is separated from other spaces or passageways by interior walls; moreover, it is separated from outdoor areas by an exterior wall, sometimes with a door. Historically the use of Rooms dates at least to early Minoan cultures about 2200 BC, where excavations on Santorini, Greece at Akrotiri reveal clearly defined Rooms within certain structures.
Millennium Development Goals	The Millennium Development Goals are eight international development goals that all 192 United Nations member states and at least 23 international organizations have agreed to achieve by the year 2015. They include reducing extreme poverty, reducing child mortality rates, fighting disease epidemics such as AIDS, and developing a global partnership for development.
	In 2001, recognizing the need to assist impoverished nations more aggressively, UN member states adopted the targets. The Millennium Development Goalss aim to spur development by improving social and economic conditions in the world`s poorest countries.
Consumer Protection	Consumer protection laws are designed to ensure fair competition and the free flow of truthful information in the marketplace. The laws are designed to prevent businesses that engage in fraud or specified unfair practices from gaining an advantage over competitors and may provide additional protection for the weak and those unable to take care of themselves. Consumer protection laws are a form of government regulation which aim to protect the interests of consumers.
Sustainable consumption	Definitions of Sustainable consumption share a number of common features, and to an extent build in the characteristics of sustainable production, its twin sister concept and inherit much of from the idea of sustainable development:
	· Quality of life;
	· Wise use of resources, and minimisation of waste and pollution;
	· Use of renewable resources within their capacity for renewal;
	· Fuller product life-cycles; and
	· Intergenerational and intragenerational equity

The definition proposed by the 1994 Oslo Symposium on Sustainable consumption defines it as `the use of services and related products which respond to basic needs and bring a better quality of life while minimising the use of natural resources and toxic materials as well as emissions of waste and pollutants over the life cycle of the service or product so as not to jeopardise the needs of future generations.`

The Centre on Sustainable consumption and Production is one leading independent authority, that is exploring the dimensions of consumption and production. Perhaps controversially Tesco, the largest supermarket in the United Kingdom, announced in 2007 a Â£5m project to create a Sustainable consumption Institute (SCI).

Sustainable consumption is not always equivalent to livable conditions.

Consumer privacy

Consumer privacy laws and regulations seek to protect any individual from loss of privacy due to failures or limitations of corporate customer privacy measures. They recognize that the damage done by privacy loss is typically not measurable, nor can it be undone, and that commercial organizations have little or no interest in taking unprofitable measures to drastically increase privacy of customers - indeed, their motivation is very often quite the opposite, to share data for commercial advantage, and to fail to officially recognize it as sensitive, so as to avoid legal liability for lapses of security that may occur.

Consumer privacy concerns date back to the first commercial couriers and bankers, who in every culture took strong measures to protect customer privacy, but also in every culture tended to be subject to very harsh punitive measures for failures to keep a customer`s information private.

Predatory pricing

In business and economics, Predatory pricing is the practice of selling a product or service at a very low price, intending to drive competitors out of the market, or create barriers to entry for potential new competitors. If competitors or potential competitors cannot sustain equal or lower prices without losing money, they go out of business or choose not to enter the business. The predatory merchant then has fewer competitors or is even a de facto monopoly, and hypothetically could then raise prices above what the market would otherwise bear.

Chapter 8. Consumers and business ethics

Price fixing	Price fixing is an agreement between participants on the same side in a market to buy or sell a product, service, or commodity only at a fixed price, or maintain the market conditions such that the price is maintained at a given level by controlling supply and demand. The group of market makers involved in Price fixing is sometimes referred to as a cartel. Price fixing may be intended to push the price of a product as high as possible, leading to profits for all sellers, but it may also have the goal to fix, peg, discount, or stabilize prices.
Consumerism	Consumerism is social and economic order that is based on the systematic creation and fostering of a desire to purchase goods or services in ever greater amounts. The term is often associated with criticisms of consumption starting with Thorstein Veblen or, more recently by a movement called Enoughism. Veblen`s subject of examination, the newly emergent middle class arising at the turn of the twentieth century, comes to full fruition by the end of the twentieth century through the process of globalization.
Fordism	Fordism refers to various social theories about production and related socio-economic phenomena. It has varying but related meanings in different fields, as well as for Marxist and non-Marxist scholars. The essential meaning is that the worker must be paid higher wages in order to afford the products that the industrialist himself produces, causing an economy that runs full-circle.
Consequentialism	Consequentialism refers to those moral theories which hold that the consequences of a particular action form the basis for any valid moral judgment about that action . Thus, from a consequentialist standpoint, a morally right action is one that produces a good outcome, or consequence. This view is often expressed as the aphorism `The ends justify the means`.
Consumer sovereignty	Consumer sovereignty is a term which is used in economics to refer to the rule or sovereignty of consumers in markets as to production of goods. It is the power of consumers to decide what gets produced. People use this term to describe the consumer as the `king,` or ruler, of the market, the one who determines what products will be produced.
Sweatshop	Sweatshop is a working environment considered to be unacceptably difficult or dangerous -- particularly by industrialized nations with high standards of living. However Sweatshops may exist in any country. Sweatshop workers often work long hours for unusually low pay, regardless of laws mandating overtime pay or a minimum wage.

Chapter 8. Consumers and business ethics

Universal Declaration of Human Rights	The Universal Declaration of Human Rights is a declaration adopted by the United Nations General Assembly on 10 December 1948 at the Palais de Chaillot in Paris. The Declaration has been translated into at least 375 languages and dialects, making it the most widely translated document in the world. The Declaration arose directly from the experience of the Second World War and represents the first global expression of rights to which all human beings are entitled.
Fair trade	Fair trade is an organized social movement and market-based approach that aims to help producers in developing countries obtain better trading conditions and promote sustainability. The movement advocates the payment of a higher price to producers as well as social and environmental standards. It focuses in particular on exports from developing countries to developed countries, most notably handicrafts, coffee, cocoa, sugar, tea, bananas, honey, cotton, wine, fresh fruit, chocolate and flowers.
Corporate social responsibility	Corporate social responsibility also known as corporate responsibility, corporate citizenship, responsible business, sustainable responsible business (SRB), or corporate social performance, is a form of corporate self-regulation integrated into a business model. Ideally, Corporate social responsibility policy would function as a built-in, self-regulating mechanism whereby business would monitor and ensure its support to law, ethical standards, and international norms. Consequently, business would embrace responsibility for the impact of its activities on the environment, consumers, employees, communities, stakeholders and all other members of the public sphere.
Sustainable tourism	Sustainable tourism is an industry committed to making a low impact on the environment and local culture, while helping to generate future employment for local people.The positive of Sustainable tourism is to ensure that development is a positive experience for local people; tourism companies; and tourists themselves. But Sustainable tourism is not the same as ecotourism. Global economists forecast continuing international tourism growth, ranging between three and six percent annually, depending on the location.
Ecological footprint	The Ecological footprint is a measure of human demand on the Earth`s ecosystems. It compares human demand with planet Earth`s ecological capacity to regenerate. It represents the amount of biologically productive land and sea area needed to regenerate the resources a human population consumes and to absorb and render harmless the corresponding waste.

Kyoto Protocol

The Kyoto Protocol is a protocol to the United Nations Framework Convention on Climate Change (UNFCCC or FCCC), aimed at fighting global warming. The UNFCCC is an international environmental treaty with the goal of achieving `stabilization of greenhouse gas concentrations in the atmosphere at a level that would prevent dangerous anthropogenic interference with the climate system.`

The Protocol was initially adopted on 11 December 1997 in Kyoto, Japan and entered into force on 16 February 2005. As of November 2009, 187 states have signed and ratified the protocol.

Under the Protocol, 37 industrialized countries commit themselves to a reduction of four greenhouse gases (GHG) (carbon dioxide, methane, nitrous oxide, sulphur hexafluoride) and two groups of gases produced by them, and all member countries give general commitments.

Chapter 9. Suppliers, competitors, and business ethics

Millennium Development Goals	The Millennium Development Goals are eight international development goals that all 192 United Nations member states and at least 23 international organizations have agreed to achieve by the year 2015. They include reducing extreme poverty, reducing child mortality rates, fighting disease epidemics such as AIDS, and developing a global partnership for development. In 2001, recognizing the need to assist impoverished nations more aggressively, UN member states adopted the targets. The Millennium Development Goalss aim to spur development by improving social and economic conditions in the world`s poorest countries.
Resource dependence theory	Resource dependence theory is the study of how the external resources of organizations affects the behavior of the organization. The procurement of external resources is an important tenet of both the strategic and tactical management of any company. Nevertheless, a theory of the consequences of this importance was not formalized until the 1970s, with the publication of The External Control of Organizations: A Resource Dependence Perspective (Pfeffer and Salancik 1978).
Consequentialism	Consequentialism refers to those moral theories which hold that the consequences of a particular action form the basis for any valid moral judgment about that action . Thus, from a consequentialist standpoint, a morally right action is one that produces a good outcome, or consequence. This view is often expressed as the aphorism `The ends justify the means`.
Supply chain	A Supply chain is a system of organizations, people, technology, activities, information and resources involved in moving a product or service from supplier to customer. Supply chain activities transform natural resources, raw materials and components into a finished product that is delivered to the end customer. In sophisticated Supply chain systems, used products may re-enter the Supply chain at any point where residual value is recyclable.
Procedural justice	Procedural justice refers to the idea of fairness in the processes that resolve disputes and allocate resources. One aspect of Procedural justice is related to discussions of the administration of justice and legal proceedings. This sense of Procedural justice is connected to due process (U.S)., fundamental justice (Canada), procedural fairness (Australia) and natural justice (other Common law jurisdictions), but the idea of Procedural justice can also be applied to nonlegal contexts in which some process is employed to resolve conflict or divide benefits or burdens.

Chapter 9. Suppliers, competitors, and business ethics

Industrial espionage	Industrial espionage, economic espionage or corporate espionage is espionage conducted for commercial purposes instead of purely national security purposes. Economic espionage is conducted or orchestrated by governments and is international in scope, while industrial or corporate espionage is more often national and occurs between companies or corporations. `Competitive intelligence` describes the legal and ethical activity of systematically gathering, analyzing and managing information on industrial competitors.
Intellectual property	Intellectual property is a term referring to a number of distinct types of creations of the mind for which property rights are recognised--and the corresponding fields of law. Under Intellectual property law, owners are granted certain exclusive rights to a variety of intangible assets, such as musical, literary, and artistic works; discoveries and inventions; and words, phrases, symbols, and designs. Common types of Intellectual property include copyrights, trademarks, patents, industrial design rights and trade secrets in some jurisdictions.
Dirty trick	Dirty tricks are unethical, duplicitous, slanderous or illegal tactics employed to destroy or diminish the effectiveness of political or business opponents. The term `Dirty trick` can also be used to refer to an underhanded technique to get ahead of an opponent (such as sabotage or disregarding rules of engagement). Leaking secret information, digging into a candidate`s past (opposition research) or exposing real conflicts between the image presented and the person behind the image are always subject to argument as to whether they are Dirty tricks or truth-telling.
Predatory pricing	In business and economics, Predatory pricing is the practice of selling a product or service at a very low price, intending to drive competitors out of the market, or create barriers to entry for potential new competitors. If competitors or potential competitors cannot sustain equal or lower prices without losing money, they go out of business or choose not to enter the business. The predatory merchant then has fewer competitors or is even a de facto monopoly, and hypothetically could then raise prices above what the market would otherwise bear.
Cartel	A Cartel is a formal (explicit) agreement among competing firms. It is a formal organization of producers and manufacturers that agree to fix prices, marketing, and production. Cartels usually occur in an oligopolistic industry, where there is a small number of sellers and usually involve homogeneous products.

79

Chapter 9. Suppliers, competitors, and business ethics

Bribery	Bribery, a form of corruption, is an act implying money or gift given that alters the behavior of the recipient. Bribery constitutes a crime and is defined by Black's Law Dictionary as the offering, giving, receiving, or soliciting of any item of value to influence the actions of an official or other person in charge of a public or legal duty. The bribe is the gift bestowed to influence the recipient's conduct.
Business ethics	Business ethics is a form of applied ethics or professional ethics that examines ethical principles and moral or ethical problems that arise in a business environment. It applies to all aspects of business conduct and is relevant to the conduct of individuals and business organizations as a whole. Applied ethics is a field of ethics that deals with ethical questions in many fields such as medical, technical, legal and Business ethics.
Kyoto Protocol	The Kyoto Protocol is a protocol to the United Nations Framework Convention on Climate Change (UNFCCC or FCCC), aimed at fighting global warming. The UNFCCC is an international environmental treaty with the goal of achieving 'stabilization of greenhouse gas concentrations in the atmosphere at a level that would prevent dangerous anthropogenic interference with the climate system.'

The Protocol was initially adopted on 11 December 1997 in Kyoto, Japan and entered into force on 16 February 2005. As of November 2009, 187 states have signed and ratified the protocol.

Under the Protocol, 37 industrialized countries commit themselves to a reduction of four greenhouse gases (GHG) (carbon dioxide, methane, nitrous oxide, sulphur hexafluoride) and two groups of gases produced by them, and all member countries give general commitments. |
| Public Interest | The Public interest refers to the 'common well-being' or 'general welfare.' The Public interest is central to policy debates, politics, democracy and the nature of government itself. While nearly everyone claims that aiding the common well-being or general welfare is positive, there is little, if any, consensus on what exactly constitutes the Public interest.

There are different views on how many members of the public must benefit from an action before it can be declared to be in the Public interest: at one extreme, an action has to benefit every single member of society in order to be truly in the Public interest; at the other extreme, any action can be in the Public interest as long as it benefits some of the population and harms none. |

Chapter 9. Suppliers, competitors, and business ethics

Race to the bottom	A Race to the bottom is a socio-economic concept that is argued to occur between countries as an outcome of regulatory competition. When competition becomes fierce between nations over a particular area of trade and production, countries are given increased incentive to dismantle currently existing regulatory standards. A Race to the bottom may also occur within a country (such as between states or counties), but this occurs much less frequently because the federal government has recourse to enact legislation slowing or halting the race before its effects become too pervasive.
Sweatshop	Sweatshop is a working environment considered to be unacceptably difficult or dangerous -- particularly by industrialized nations with high standards of living. However Sweatshops may exist in any country. Sweatshop workers often work long hours for unusually low pay, regardless of laws mandating overtime pay or a minimum wage.
Trade union	A Trade union or labor union is an organization of workers who have banded together to achieve common goals such as better working conditions. The Trade union, through its leadership, bargains with the employer on behalf of union members (rank and file members) and negotiates labour contracts (collective bargaining) with employers. This may include the negotiation of wages, work rules, complaint procedures, rules governing hiring, firing and promotion of workers, benefits, workplace safety and policies.
Fair trade	Fair trade is an organized social movement and market-based approach that aims to help producers in developing countries obtain better trading conditions and promote sustainability. The movement advocates the payment of a higher price to producers as well as social and environmental standards. It focuses in particular on exports from developing countries to developed countries, most notably handicrafts, coffee, cocoa, sugar, tea, bananas, honey, cotton, wine, fresh fruit, chocolate and flowers.
Room	A Room, in architecture, is any distinguishable space within a structure. Usually, a Room is separated from other spaces or passageways by interior walls; moreover, it is separated from outdoor areas by an exterior wall, sometimes with a door. Historically the use of Rooms dates at least to early Minoan cultures about 2200 BC, where excavations on Santorini, Greece at Akrotiri reveal clearly defined Rooms within certain structures.
Ecosystem	An Ecosystem consists of all the organisms living in a particular area, as well as all the nonliving, physical components of the environment with which the organisms interact, such as air, soil, water, and sunlight. It is all the organisms in a given area, along with the nonliving (abiotic) factors with which they interact; a biological community and its physical environment. The entire array of organisms inhabiting a particular Ecosystem is called a community.

Chapter 9. Suppliers, competitors, and business ethics

Sustainable consumption	Definitions of Sustainable consumption share a number of common features, and to an extent build in the characteristics of sustainable production, its twin sister concept and inherit much of from the idea of sustainable development:
	· Quality of life;
	· Wise use of resources, and minimisation of waste and pollution;
	· Use of renewable resources within their capacity for renewal;
	· Fuller product life-cycles; and
	· Intergenerational and intragenerational equity
	The definition proposed by the 1994 Oslo Symposium on Sustainable consumption defines it as `the use of services and related products which respond to basic needs and bring a better quality of life while minimising the use of natural resources and toxic materials as well as emissions of waste and pollutants over the life cycle of the service or product so as not to jeopardise the needs of future generations.`
	The Centre on Sustainable consumption and Production is one leading independent authority, that is exploring the dimensions of consumption and production. Perhaps controversially Tesco, the largest supermarket in the United Kingdom, announced in 2007 a Â£5m project to create a Sustainable consumption Institute (SCI).
	Sustainable consumption is not always equivalent to livable conditions.
Organization	An Organization is a social arrangement which pursues collective goals, controls its own performance, and has a boundary separating it from its environment. The word itself is derived from the Greek word organon, itself derived from the better-known word ergon.
	In the social sciences, Organizations are the object of analysis for a number of disciplines, such as sociology, economics, political science, psychology, management, and Organizational communication.

Chapter 10. Civil society and business ethics

Organization	An Organization is a social arrangement which pursues collective goals, controls its own performance, and has a boundary separating it from its environment. The word itself is derived from the Greek word organon, itself derived from the better-known word ergon.
	In the social sciences, Organizations are the object of analysis for a number of disciplines, such as sociology, economics, political science, psychology, management, and Organizational communication.
Kyoto Protocol	The Kyoto Protocol is a protocol to the United Nations Framework Convention on Climate Change (UNFCCC or FCCC), aimed at fighting global warming. The UNFCCC is an international environmental treaty with the goal of achieving `stabilization of greenhouse gas concentrations in the atmosphere at a level that would prevent dangerous anthropogenic interference with the climate system.`
	The Protocol was initially adopted on 11 December 1997 in Kyoto, Japan and entered into force on 16 February 2005. As of November 2009, 187 states have signed and ratified the protocol.
	Under the Protocol, 37 industrialized countries commit themselves to a reduction of four greenhouse gases (GHG) (carbon dioxide, methane, nitrous oxide, sulphur hexafluoride) and two groups of gases produced by them, and all member countries give general commitments.
Trade union	A Trade union or labor union is an organization of workers who have banded together to achieve common goals such as better working conditions. The Trade union, through its leadership, bargains with the employer on behalf of union members (rank and file members) and negotiates labour contracts (collective bargaining) with employers. This may include the negotiation of wages, work rules, complaint procedures, rules governing hiring, firing and promotion of workers, benefits, workplace safety and policies.
Universal Declaration of Human Rights	The Universal Declaration of Human Rights is a declaration adopted by the United Nations General Assembly on 10 December 1948 at the Palais de Chaillot in Paris. The Declaration has been translated into at least 375 languages and dialects, making it the most widely translated document in the world. The Declaration arose directly from the experience of the Second World War and represents the first global expression of rights to which all human beings are entitled.

Chapter 10. Civil society and business ethics

Utilitarianism	Utilitarianism is the idea that the moral worth of an action is determined solely by its utility in providing happiness or pleasure as summed among all sentient beings. It is thus a form of consequentialism, meaning that the moral worth of an action is determined by its outcome. The most influential contributors to this ideology were Jeremy Bentham and John Stuart Mill.
Trust	In common law legal systems, a trust is a relationship whereby property (including real, tangible and intangible) is managed by one person for the benefit of another. A trust is created by a settlor (or feoffor to uses), who entrusts some or all of their property to people of their choice (the trustees or feoffee to uses). The trustees hold legal title to the trust property (or trust corpus), but they are obliged to hold the property for the benefit of one or more individuals or organizations (the beneficiary, cestui que use, or cestui que trust), usually specified by the settlor, who hold equitable title.
Stakeholder management	The importance of Stakeholder management is to support an organization in achieving its strategic objectives by interpreting and influencing both the external and internal environments and by creating positive relationships with stakeholders through the appropriate management of their expectations and agreed objectives. Stakeholder management is a process and control that must be planned and guided by underlying Principles.
Consequentialism	Consequentialism refers to those moral theories which hold that the consequences of a particular action form the basis for any valid moral judgment about that action . Thus, from a consequentialist standpoint, a morally right action is one that produces a good outcome, or consequence. This view is often expressed as the aphorism `The ends justify the means`.
Supply chain	A Supply chain is a system of organizations, people, technology, activities, information and resources involved in moving a product or service from supplier to customer. Supply chain activities transform natural resources, raw materials and components into a finished product that is delivered to the end customer. In sophisticated Supply chain systems, used products may re-enter the Supply chain at any point where residual value is recyclable.
Discourse ethics	Discourse ethics refers to a type of argument that attempts to establish normative or ethical truths by examining the presuppositions of discourse. German philosophers Jürgen Habermas and Karl-Otto Apel are probably properly considered as the originators of modern Discourse ethics. Habermas`s Discourse ethics is his attempt to explain the implications of communicative rationality in the sphere of moral insight and normative validity.

Chapter 10. Civil society and business ethics

Room	A Room, in architecture, is any distinguishable space within a structure. Usually, a Room is separated from other spaces or passageways by interior walls; moreover, it is separated from outdoor areas by an exterior wall, sometimes with a door. Historically the use of Rooms dates at least to early Minoan cultures about 2200 BC, where excavations on Santorini, Greece at Akrotiri reveal clearly defined Rooms within certain structures.
Environmental management	Environmental management is not, as the phrase could suggest, the management of the environment as such, but rather the management of interaction by the modern human societies with, and impact upon the environment. The three main issues that affect managers are those involving politics (networking), programs (projects), and resources (money, facilities, etc).. The need for Environmental management can be viewed from a variety of perspectives.
Triple bottom line	The Triple bottom line captures an expanded spectrum of values and criteria for measuring organizational (and societal) success: economic, ecological and social. With the ratification of the United Nations and ICLEI Triple bottom line standard for urban and community accounting in early 2007, this became the dominant approach to public sector full cost accounting. Similar UN standards apply to natural capital and human capital measurement to assist in measurements required by Triple bottom line, e.g. the ecoBudget standard for reporting ecological footprint.
Corporate social responsibility	Corporate social responsibility also known as corporate responsibility, corporate citizenship, responsible business, sustainable responsible business (SRB), or corporate social performance, is a form of corporate self-regulation integrated into a business model. Ideally, Corporate social responsibility policy would function as a built-in, self-regulating mechanism whereby business would monitor and ensure its support to law, ethical standards, and international norms. Consequently, business would embrace responsibility for the impact of its activities on the environment, consumers, employees, communities, stakeholders and all other members of the public sphere.

Go to **Cram101.com** for Interactive Practice Exams for this book or virtually any of your books.
And, **NEVER** highlight a book again!

Chapter 11. Government regulation, and business ethics

Kyoto Protocol	The Kyoto Protocol is a protocol to the United Nations Framework Convention on Climate Change (UNFCCC or FCCC), aimed at fighting global warming. The UNFCCC is an international environmental treaty with the goal of achieving `stabilization of greenhouse gas concentrations in the atmosphere at a level that would prevent dangerous anthropogenic interference with the climate system.` The Protocol was initially adopted on 11 December 1997 in Kyoto, Japan and entered into force on 16 February 2005. As of November 2009, 187 states have signed and ratified the protocol. Under the Protocol, 37 industrialized countries commit themselves to a reduction of four greenhouse gases (GHG) (carbon dioxide, methane, nitrous oxide, sulphur hexafluoride) and two groups of gases produced by them, and all member countries give general commitments.
Mergers and acquisitions	The phrase Mergers and acquisitions refers to the aspect of corporate strategy, corporate finance and management dealing with the buying, selling and combining of different companies that can aid, finance, or help a growing company in a given industry grow rapidly without having to create another business entity. An acquisition, also known as a takeover or a buyout, is the buying of one company (the `target`) by another. Consolidation is when two companies combine together to form a new company alltogether.
Consumer protection	Consumer protection laws are designed to ensure fair competition and the free flow of truthful information in the marketplace. The laws are designed to prevent businesses that engage in fraud or specified unfair practices from gaining an advantage over competitors and may provide additional protection for the weak and those unable to take care of themselves. Consumer protection laws are a form of government regulation which aim to protect the interests of consumers.
Organization	An Organization is a social arrangement which pursues collective goals, controls its own performance, and has a boundary separating it from its environment. The word itself is derived from the Greek word organon, itself derived from the better-known word ergon. In the social sciences, Organizations are the object of analysis for a number of disciplines, such as sociology, economics, political science, psychology, management, and Organizational communication.

Clam101

Chapter 11. Government regulation, and business ethics

Bribery	Bribery, a form of corruption, is an act implying money or gift given that alters the behavior of the recipient. Bribery constitutes a crime and is defined by Black's Law Dictionary as the offering, giving, receiving, or soliciting of any item of value to influence the actions of an official or other person in charge of a public or legal duty. The bribe is the gift bestowed to influence the recipient's conduct.
Insider trading	Insider trading is the trading of a corporation's stock or other securities (e.g. bonds or stock options) by individuals with potential access to non-public information about the company. In most countries, trading by corporate insiders such as officers, key employees, directors, and large shareholders may be legal, if this trading is done in a way that does not take advantage of non-public information. However, the term is frequently used to refer to a practice in which an insider or a related party trades based on material non-public information obtained during the performance of the insider's duties at the corporation, or otherwise in breach of a fiduciary or other relationship of trust and confidence or where the non-public information was misappropriated from the company.
Trade union	A Trade union or labor union is an organization of workers who have banded together to achieve common goals such as better working conditions. The Trade union, through its leadership, bargains with the employer on behalf of union members (rank and file members) and negotiates labour contracts (collective bargaining) with employers. This may include the negotiation of wages, work rules, complaint procedures, rules governing hiring, firing and promotion of workers, benefits, workplace safety and policies.
Universal Declaration of Human Rights	The Universal Declaration of Human Rights is a declaration adopted by the United Nations General Assembly on 10 December 1948 at the Palais de Chaillot in Paris. The Declaration has been translated into at least 375 languages and dialects, making it the most widely translated document in the world. The Declaration arose directly from the experience of the Second World War and represents the first global expression of rights to which all human beings are entitled.
Utilitarianism	Utilitarianism is the idea that the moral worth of an action is determined solely by its utility in providing happiness or pleasure as summed among all sentient beings. It is thus a form of consequentialism, meaning that the moral worth of an action is determined by its outcome. The most influential contributors to this ideology were Jeremy Bentham and John Stuart Mill.
Stakeholder management	The importance of Stakeholder management is to support an organization in achieving its strategic objectives by interpreting and influencing both the external and internal environments and by creating positive relationships with stakeholders through the appropriate management of their expectations and agreed objectives. Stakeholder management is a process and control that must be planned and guided by underlying Principles.

Chapter 11. Government regulation, and business ethics

Procedural justice	Procedural justice refers to the idea of fairness in the processes that resolve disputes and allocate resources. One aspect of Procedural justice is related to discussions of the administration of justice and legal proceedings. This sense of Procedural justice is connected to due process (U.S)., fundamental justice (Canada), procedural fairness (Australia) and natural justice (other Common law jurisdictions), but the idea of Procedural justice can also be applied to nonlegal contexts in which some process is employed to resolve conflict or divide benefits or burdens.
Room	A Room, in architecture, is any distinguishable space within a structure. Usually, a Room is separated from other spaces or passageways by interior walls; moreover, it is separated from outdoor areas by an exterior wall, sometimes with a door. Historically the use of Rooms dates at least to early Minoan cultures about 2200 BC, where excavations on Santorini, Greece at Akrotiri reveal clearly defined Rooms within certain structures.
Public Interest	The Public interest refers to the `common well-being` or `general welfare.` The Public interest is central to policy debates, politics, democracy and the nature of government itself. While nearly everyone claims that aiding the common well-being or general welfare is positive, there is little, if any, consensus on what exactly constitutes the Public interest.
	There are different views on how many members of the public must benefit from an action before it can be declared to be in the Public interest: at one extreme, an action has to benefit every single member of society in order to be truly in the Public interest; at the other extreme, any action can be in the Public interest as long as it benefits some of the population and harms none.
Environmental management	Environmental management is not, as the phrase could suggest, the management of the environment as such, but rather the management of interaction by the modern human societies with, and impact upon the environment. The three main issues that affect managers are those involving politics (networking), programs (projects), and resources (money, facilities, etc).. The need for Environmental management can be viewed from a variety of perspectives.
Race to the bottom	A Race to the bottom is a socio-economic concept that is argued to occur between countries as an outcome of regulatory competition. When competition becomes fierce between nations over a particular area of trade and production, countries are given increased incentive to dismantle currently existing regulatory standards.

Chapter 11. Government regulation, and business ethics

	A Race to the bottom may also occur within a country (such as between states or counties), but this occurs much less frequently because the federal government has recourse to enact legislation slowing or halting the race before its effects become too pervasive.
Supply chain	A Supply chain is a system of organizations, people, technology, activities, information and resources involved in moving a product or service from supplier to customer. Supply chain activities transform natural resources, raw materials and components into a finished product that is delivered to the end customer. In sophisticated Supply chain systems, used products may re-enter the Supply chain at any point where residual value is recyclable.
Corporate social responsibility	Corporate social responsibility also known as corporate responsibility, corporate citizenship, responsible business, sustainable responsible business (SRB), or corporate social performance, is a form of corporate self-regulation integrated into a business model. Ideally, Corporate social responsibility policy would function as a built-in, self-regulating mechanism whereby business would monitor and ensure its support to law, ethical standards, and international norms. Consequently, business would embrace responsibility for the impact of its activities on the environment, consumers, employees, communities, stakeholders and all other members of the public sphere.
Polder model	The Polder Model is a term with uncertain origin that was first used to describe the internationally acclaimed Dutch version of consensus policy in economics, specifically in the 1980s and 1990s. However, the term was quickly adopted for a much wider meaning, for similar cases of consensus decision-making, which are supposedly typically Dutch. It is described with phrases like `a pragmatic recognition of pluriformity` and `cooperation despite differences`.
Sustainable development	Sustainable development is a pattern of resource use that aims to meet human needs while preserving the environment so that these needs can be met not only in the present, but also for future generations. The term was used by the Brundtland Commission which coined what has become the most often-quoted definition of Sustainable development as development that `meets the needs of the present without compromising the ability of future generations to meet their own needs.`
	Sustainable development ties together concern for the carrying capacity of natural systems with the social challenges facing humanity. As early as the 1970s `sustainability` was employed to describe an economy `in equilibrium with basic ecological support systems.` Ecologists have pointed to The Limits to Growth, and presented the alternative of a `steady state economy` in order to address environmental concerns.

Chapter 11. Government regulation, and business ethics

| Sustainability | Sustainability is the capacity to endure. In ecology the word describes how biological systems remain diverse and productive over time. For humans it is the potential for long-term maintenance of well being, which in turn depends on the well being of the natural world and the responsible use of natural resources. |

Chapter 12. Conclusions and future perspectives

Business ethics	Business ethics is a form of applied ethics or professional ethics that examines ethical principles and moral or ethical problems that arise in a business environment. It applies to all aspects of business conduct and is relevant to the conduct of individuals and business organizations as a whole. Applied ethics is a field of ethics that deals with ethical questions in many fields such as medical, technical, legal and Business ethics.
Ecosystem	An Ecosystem consists of all the organisms living in a particular area, as well as all the nonliving, physical components of the environment with which the organisms interact, such as air, soil, water, and sunlight. It is all the organisms in a given area, along with the nonliving (abiotic) factors with which they interact; a biological community and its physical environment. The entire array of organisms inhabiting a particular Ecosystem is called a community.
Sustainability	Sustainability is the capacity to endure. In ecology the word describes how biological systems remain diverse and productive over time. For humans it is the potential for long-term maintenance of well being, which in turn depends on the well being of the natural world and the responsible use of natural resources.
Triple bottom line	The Triple bottom line captures an expanded spectrum of values and criteria for measuring organizational (and societal) success: economic, ecological and social. With the ratification of the United Nations and ICLEI Triple bottom line standard for urban and community accounting in early 2007, this became the dominant approach to public sector full cost accounting. Similar UN standards apply to natural capital and human capital measurement to assist in measurements required by Triple bottom line, e.g. the ecoBudget standard for reporting ecological footprint.
Work-life balance	Work-life balance is a broad concept including proper prioritizing between `work` (career and ambition) on one hand and `life` (pleasure, leisure, family and spiritual development) on the other. Related, though broader, terms include `lifestyle balance` and `life balance`. The expression was first used in the late 1970s to describe the balance between an individual`s work and personal life.
Kyoto Protocol	The Kyoto Protocol is a protocol to the United Nations Framework Convention on Climate Change (UNFCCC or FCCC), aimed at fighting global warming. The UNFCCC is an international environmental treaty with the goal of achieving `stabilization of greenhouse gas concentrations in the atmosphere at a level that would prevent dangerous anthropogenic interference with the climate system.`

103

Chapter 12. Conclusions and future perspectives

	The Protocol was initially adopted on 11 December 1997 in Kyoto, Japan and entered into force on 16 February 2005. As of November 2009, 187 states have signed and ratified the protocol.
	Under the Protocol, 37 industrialized countries commit themselves to a reduction of four greenhouse gases (GHG) (carbon dioxide, methane, nitrous oxide, sulphur hexafluoride) and two groups of gases produced by them, and all member countries give general commitments.
Corporate social responsibility	Corporate social responsibility also known as corporate responsibility, corporate citizenship, responsible business, sustainable responsible business (SRB), or corporate social performance, is a form of corporate self-regulation integrated into a business model. Ideally, Corporate social responsibility policy would function as a built-in, self-regulating mechanism whereby business would monitor and ensure its support to law, ethical standards, and international norms. Consequently, business would embrace responsibility for the impact of its activities on the environment, consumers, employees, communities, stakeholders and all other members of the public sphere.
Organization	An Organization is a social arrangement which pursues collective goals, controls its own performance, and has a boundary separating it from its environment. The word itself is derived from the Greek word organon, itself derived from the better-known word ergon.
	In the social sciences, Organizations are the object of analysis for a number of disciplines, such as sociology, economics, political science, psychology, management, and Organizational communication.
Room	A Room, in architecture, is any distinguishable space within a structure. Usually, a Room is separated from other spaces or passageways by interior walls; moreover, it is separated from outdoor areas by an exterior wall, sometimes with a door. Historically the use of Rooms dates at least to early Minoan cultures about 2200 BC, where excavations on Santorini, Greece at Akrotiri reveal clearly defined Rooms within certain structures.
Universal Declaration of Human Rights	The Universal Declaration of Human Rights is a declaration adopted by the United Nations General Assembly on 10 December 1948 at the Palais de Chaillot in Paris. The Declaration has been translated into at least 375 languages and dialects, making it the most widely translated document in the world. The Declaration arose directly from the experience of the Second World War and represents the first global expression of rights to which all human beings are entitled.

Chapter 12. Conclusions and future perspectives

Bribery	Bribery, a form of corruption, is an act implying money or gift given that alters the behavior of the recipient. Bribery constitutes a crime and is defined by Black`s Law Dictionary as the offering, giving, receiving, or soliciting of any item of value to influence the actions of an official or other person in charge of a public or legal duty. The bribe is the gift bestowed to influence the recipient`s conduct.
Fair trade	Fair trade is an organized social movement and market-based approach that aims to help producers in developing countries obtain better trading conditions and promote sustainability. The movement advocates the payment of a higher price to producers as well as social and environmental standards. It focuses in particular on exports from developing countries to developed countries, most notably handicrafts, coffee, cocoa, sugar, tea, bananas, honey, cotton, wine, fresh fruit, chocolate and flowers.

Lightning Source UK Ltd.
Milton Keynes UK
UKOW07f0707171015

260777UK00004B/72/P

9 781428 883611